How To Treat Your Wife: A Book For Men

Orlando Alonso

Contents

1. Introduction — 3
2. Anger — 7
3. Wife — 11
4. How not to flip out on your wife — 15
5. The Lecture Problem — 18
6. The Marriage-Killer — 22
7. Showing Love — 26
8. The WIIFM — 28
9. Numero #1 — 29
10. Hobby — 30
11. Working Out — 30
12. RE: Cheating — 33
13. Let's Wrap It Up! — 35

1. Introduction

     You're probably reading this book because your family life isn't turning out the way you imagined it would. Heck it might even suck. When work ends and you know it's time to go home, you kind of don't want to go. Understandable actually. Think about it: Nagging wife, crazy kids, messy house, stuff that needs to be done around the house..so on and so on. When all you really want to do is drink a beer. It's been a long day and heck you deserve one. Problem is that being home doesn't let you do that. It's a madhouse and you wish it was just a little more sane.

     Your wife alone is driving you nuts. Every time you talk to her it ends up in an argument. It could be something as dumb as her asking, "What do you want for dinner?", and BAM things go downhill quick. You think to yourself, "What the heck happened to us? Why is she so crazy now? I'm not sure she's the same women I married." All good questions actually. Because the truth is this: Being married is freaking tough. Then add some kids to the mix and it's all out of control. Now the reason for this book is to figure out why your household is like this, and how to fix it. It's a short book and I'm sure there are a ton of other books that can really get in the weeds about this stuff. You know what though? You probably don't have time to read it. It's as thick as a Webster's Dictionary and probably written in a way that's kinda boring. Don't get me wrong there are some great books, but this book is for you. The regular guy...just like me.

     We don't have a ton of time and honestly we just want to learn what works. Have you ever noticed that a lot of those books don't tell you how to make things work? They just give you an idea of what to do. I'm not gonna do that with you. I'm basically going to give you an outline of tools that will make things better. If you use the tools in time things will get better. After a while you will actually mold the tools to make them work better for you and your circumstances.

Now here's the catch. There's two parts to this catch. The first part is this: YOU HAVE TO DO THESE OVER AND OVER AGAIN AND IT WILL NEVER END. None of what I show you in this book will work if you don't use it...duh. You can read this book and say, "What a great book." and still stay in the crapola you're in today. It will work though if you put some elbow grease in it. Nothing, let me repeat, NOTHING happens if you do nothing. Crazy huh? That's freaking deep right there. It's like going to the gym (sorry for using this example. I know it's kinda lame). If you don't go nothing happens. Also like I stated you have to do them forever. That sounds kinda like a bum rap but let me explain. After a while using the tools I show you they will become second nature to you. At first they are hard to do and you have to conscientiously do them. Once you get accustomed to them they become easier and enjoyable.

Let me use the gym example again, this is a better example though. If you go to the gym and lift a lot, within a six month timeframe you can put on a lot of muscle. With the right supplements you can get really damn big. Let's say you add about 20lbs of muscle on your body, which is really good gains. Yet at one point you might get tired of going or something else comes up. Then you only start going about twice or three times a week. You don't even lift as heavy as you used to.

The thing no one ever brings up is the fact that you are keeping real muscle on your frame. Muscle that will probably stay with you forever. So instead of keeping 20lbs of muscle you go down to 10 or 15lbs in gain.

You know what? That's pretty damn good. You've

basically changed yourself with some hard work at first and then being consistent from there on out. Also that extra muscle is not a pain in the ass to keep. You don't have to be stuffing yourself with supplements and be in the gym everyday. Just eat a little cleaner and hit the gym a couple days a week. Not too bad right? That's the same kind of goal you should have with the tools I show you.

Okay, so what's the second part of the catch? Alright be ready because this is the hard part. I'm personally a Christian. One of the parts of being a Christian is that men are the head of the household. This is what the Bible says about it, "Wives, submit to your husbands as to the Lord. For the husband is the head of the wife as Christ is the head of the church, his body, of which he is the Savior" Ephesians 5:22-23. I want to highlight the part that says "head of the wife". This also translates to being the head of the household. Sounds good right? Now let me explain.

I've met a TON of guys that use this as their way of seeing things when it comes to their house. Even non-Christians, especially in America, use this point of view. Basically they use this idea in a way that says, "I'm the head of the house and therefore it's my rules." That is completely stupid. Let me explain in a very blunt way how that verse applies to you. Now be ready because this is not going to be easy to swallow:

If there is any disarray in your house, it's your fault.

Read it again. Let it sink in. Got it? Good. So what does it really mean?

If when you get home and your wife is acting like a crazy bitch, you made her that way. Yes, YOU. Not her but you. I can hear some of you already saying, "But Orlando you don't know my wife...blah blah blah..." Look some of you really have a wife that something is clinically wrong with her. That percentage is tiny, so don't think you can use the "she's really crazy" excuse. You are the **head of the household** and therefore the way you treat her is the way she will respond. Now you see why people use that verse completely out of context??? If God made it that the man is the head of the household and you agree with that, then guess what? You also have to believe that your actions dictate how your house works. It's that plain. You can't have your cake and eat it too when it comes to that verse or way of thinking.

That's the second catch which a lot of guys have a hard time with. They want to think it's 50/50 when it comes to the relationship. To a degree that is true. But your wife is not going to give you 50% if all you're giving is 2%. If you're only giving 2% and then add to that treating her wrong, freaking fuggedabout her acting sane.

Now some of you may think, "Dude I treat her good! And she still act's like a nutball." In the chapter about showing love I'll explain what "treating her good" actually is and what it isn't. Now before we get there though we are going to look at a serious problem with men today. Anger. Let's look at that before we get to relationships.

This the intro. You think you can keep reading? Cause this stuff gets much more real as is it goes along. Just remember I'm not gonna leave you hanging.

2. Anger

You angry? Okay maybe right now you aren't but you know what I mean. That anger that just pumps through your veins seemingly for no apparent reason. It kicks in when you're at a game and someone around you is rooting against your team. What kind of an a-hole comes to your home game and starts rooting for the other team!!? How about when someone cuts you off in traffic? Don't they know you have kids in the car!! I'll take it a step further. The cell-phone company. Oh man that one right there can seriously hit the spot. Especially if you have teenagers.

Have you noticed though that sometimes you're just angry? No real reason or example for it but you just are. It gets so bad that you can't even communicate at home. Then when you try to communicate it all comes out terrible because you're angry. The even crazier part is this: You want to be angry. It fulfills you for some reason. Now I'm not some doctor that can really tell you where that anger is coming from. It's kinda of a mystery to me too. But let me share what I do know about it.

For starters men have an angry streak in them. Women don't tend to....unless you count being catty (zing!). Anyways women usually don't. Men do and it's part of who we are. It's a basic survival instinct. You have to get angry/ focused to bring down a water buffalo, fight a war, or make sure you don't get screwed. Now you see what I did there? I put "focused" as another word for angry. When men get angry we become ultra-focused. Ever been in a fight? All that anger goes right after that guy you are fighting and that is all you see. It's called tunnel vision. Once you're in tunnel vision mode you forget about everything else around you and focus on that one thing that is driving your anger. So let me be clear: Anger is not a bad thing. It's part of who we are as men and it's helped us for this long to survive.

The problem, is that anger has mutated inside us. It's not the anger that is used to survive, which is good, but instead an anger that controls us. How it got to this mutated anger I'm not entirely sure. I do believe that alcohol, drugs, and the media definitely affect it. I also know that it wells up inside of us and we want to yell at everything. The worst part is that it's for no apparent reason. It's just there ready to kickoff at any time for the most insignificant thing. It could be that your wife forgot to buy bread. Your kid picked up the drill off your workbench. Help me out here. What else? Here look, this next line is for you. Fill in the stupid thing that will set you off:

_____
_____
_____.

Alright you got one? Cool.

Like I said I'm not entirely sure how we got like this. I just know that it's affecting us. Now let me share something great with you. I'm not like that anymore. I beat it. Don't get me wrong. I do get angry but very rarely. If I do get angry it's probably for a good reason. Let me tell you the last time I got angry as an example.

I was in the middle of a match in a Brazilian Jiu-Jitsu (BJJ) tournament. I had swept the guy that I was fighting to take the top position. I literally put everything I had to sweep that guy over, which in BJJ you get two points if you sweep/throw the person over you. After about a minute I look over at the scoreboard to make sure I was winning the fight. This is what I saw: 0-0. No points at all. I was livid!! How in the heck did the ref not give me my freaking points!!! What is he blind?? So in the middle of my match, where I should have been focused on the guy that was trying to snap my arm, I start yelling at the ref for my points. Lo and behold I lost that fight (my tunnel vision switched to the ref). I was so angry at the ref that I lost my composure and the guy I was fighting got me in an armbar. That's the last time I was angry. I think it was for good reason because I was in the middle of a being competitive. The funny thing is once the match ended I cooled off and was right back to not being angry. Not even at the ref, because stuff happens, and I understand that.

You may be asking yourself, "Okay Orlando so what did you do to shut off the anger?". This is what I did; I stopped being angry. That's it. I just stopped. What made me stop was that my wife asked me, "Why do you always get so angry?" which it was hurting her also. I didn't have a good answer so I realized how futile it was to be an angry person. Ever see the movie Con-Air? In it Steve Buscemi is a serial-killer. At one point in the movie it looks like he's going to kill a little girl, because he's a serial-killer and that's what they do. She asks him, "Are you sick?" which he has an epiphany at the question and doesn't kill her. The movie makes it seem that not only does he not kill that girl but that he gets cured from being a serial-killer. Literally that how my wife's question was for me. It was a moment of enlightenment for me. Because really, WTF was I so angry about anyways? It's not like I'm getting shot at.

That really is my saying for when things get bad. We're not getting shot at, so really it's not that bad. I was in the Marine Corps and I have a bunch of friends that are still in. Right now a bunch of them are getting sent to Afghanistan. You know what?? That's were you get shot at! Now that would make me angry. Plus they don't get to see their families for months at a time, eat crappy food, maybe not even shower for weeks at a time, and sleep in the mud. Now that is something to get angry about. So why in the heck should I get angry if someone walks behind my car a little slow when I'm trying to back out? I shouldn't.

Guys, just put down the anger. Just lift that weight off your shoulders and drop it. In the chapter of "Numero #1", I'll give some insight in things to help take that weight off. In the meantime though the most important thing to do is to make a **conscience decision**. Stop being angry. It's not worth it and it's getting the better of you then you of it.

Remember: You're not getting shot at.

3. Wife

Remember when you realized that she was the one? When it hit you that she was going to be your wife? I do. We were sitting in her apartment watching TV on the couch. We weren't even talking. I don't remember what we were watching, but I know I was watching her. Amy has a steady gaze when she's interested in something so she usually doesn't notice when I sneak a peek at her. As I was looking at her I distinctly remember saying to myself, "You're gonna marry her. This is the one." I felt so in love too it was great. That was about 9 years ago.

About two years after that we were on the verge of divorce. We had only been married for about 2 years at this point. Some of you might be saying, "Damn only two years?? Heck I've been married for at least ten." This is true. Some of you are at the end of your rope and it's 10+ years, so let me explain. The reason our marriage went to the crapper so quickly is Iraq. Little confused? See when Amy and I met we were both in the Marine Corps. At the time I was finishing up my enlistment but Amy had reenlisted. This was just before Operation Iraqi Freedom. We were married for one month exactly when Amy was deployed to Iraq for eight months. She came back for about six months and then was deployed again for another six months. She spent the majority of that deployment in Fallujah, when it was its worst. Two tours pretty much back to back. That is rough on a marriage. We had to get to know each other all over again each time. That communication that we had at the beginning of our marriage got lost within that time. The deployments accelerated our marriage into a bad one.

I did not treat my wife like I should have. Instead I did what just about every guy does to his wife. I would get angry at her, lecture her for the stupidest things, and finally I ignored her. You may be reading this and realize two things. They are, "Damn that's exactly what I do." or "I don't do that." For the people that think they don't do that. Guess what? You do. Yes you do. I'll give you an example. Now before you do this little activity I must warn you. Do not get mad at your wife when you ask her this! You may not like what you hear. Instead just keep your mouth shut, say thanks for the information, and come back to the book.

Okay I want you to ask yourself this question: On a scale from 1 to 10, with 10 being the best, how would you rate your marriage? Most guys say anywhere between a 7-10. Now, remember what I said about not getting mad at your wife, go ask her the same question. Brace yourself, because you are gonna be in for a surprise. She'll probably say 2 to 6. Not what you thought **at all**. How in the heck can she think that? I mean you're a great guy! You work your ass off to pay for the house, put food on the table, and let her buy all kinds of stuff! WTF?? How can she say such a low number???

Let me tell you why. Many guys are complacent in their marriage. They think, "well this sucks, but it's life so oh well." We think that since we pay the bills and provide our wives with a good life financially, we're good husbands. So that's why we think our marriages are 7-10. Wives on the other hand need to be provided for much more than just financially. We as husbands need to invest our time into them. While were paying the bills, we ignore everything else going on around us and our wives are starving for attention. This is why she thinks the marriage is only 2-6. See, you've been lied to your whole life on what a husband is supposed to do!

Okay maybe lied to is not the best word. How about "ignorant"? I personally have always liked the word "ignorant". Simply because it means: I don't know. I'm ignorant on all kinds of stuff. Carpentry? I barely know how to use sandpaper. Sailing? All I know is how to put on a lifejacket. I don't know jack about a ton of stuff and that makes me ignorant. I can live with that, because it lets me know there is a lot left to learn. Anyways, so yeah you're ignorant. Completely ignorant on how to be married. Truth is many of you never had a good example to learn from, including me. My parents got divorced when I was thirteen. They were always fighting and my Dad (who I love very much but just let me get through this part) had no clue how to be married to my mom. So how in the heck would I know how to be married?? To a degree you have also been lied to. The lying part comes from the media. We watch love stories or hear songs about love and think (really believe actually) that is how love is. Basically the old, "Love conquers all!!!" romantic idea. I got one word for you: BULLSHIT.

Love is work.

That's right work. Everyday you have to make sure you don't flip out, lecture, or ignore your wife. Add to that then you have to love her in just the right way. Not just what you think how love is expressed but how SHE thinks love is expressed. It sounds like a lot, right? It can be at first but it gets easy to understand quickly. It really is like a formula. Let me use a lawn as an example. If you don't take care of your lawn it goes into disarray quickly. For this not to happen you need to do a few things. For starters water your lawn, then mow your lawn, and lastly use a weedwacker. Sometimes you might need some extra stuff if you really want to make it look great, but in general you know the formula. Kinda of the same thing with marriage, because although the grass might be greener on the other side, doesn't mean you can't make your own lawn

perfect.
        Alright you ready? Let's get to the nuts and bolts of this thing to make it work. Let's start with communication.

4. How not to flip out on your wife

Alright by now hopefully you agreed to make a decision of not getting angry for stupid things. That's the first part of not getting angry at your wife. The next part is this: Your wife is not psychic. Let me give you an example. My buddy had his wife take his truck to get tinted. When she came back from the tint shop he pretty much had limo tints on his truck, lol. Sorry I'm actually laughing about it. Ok back to the story. What do you think he did? That's right, he flipped out on her. Basically calling her stupid for doing such a thing, especially in California. You can't have tint so dark in your front windows, so he thought for sure he was going to get a ticket. Sounds like he should be pissed. Who in the heck gets limo tints for a truck where it's illegal??

Apparently my buddy's wife. Why did she do it? She did it because he never told her any better. All he said was, "Take my truck to the tint shop." and she did just that. She didn't know about tints being illegal in California, all she wanted to do was please her husband. He on the other hand did not EXPLAIN what he wanted to his wife. He just assumed that she knew. Wrong move, because his wife, nor yours, is a psychic. Your wife doesn't know what you want exactly, unless you tell her! Crazy huh?? Back to my buddy. Not only did he flip out on her, but not once did he thank her. Dude, she went to the tint shop for him, not for her benefit but his. Oh and he has never got a ticket for the tint.

Now let me show you what he should have said, "Babe, thank you. Although this is the wrong tint. That is my bad because I didn't tell you exactly what I needed. I'll probably have to take it back and get it fixed. Either way thanks. Next time I'll make sure to tell you." Remember this! This is how you should talk to your wife. You know why? Because she's a human being and deserves to be spoken to respectfully. Just because you've seen her give birth, take a crap, and had sex with her doesn't mean that you can start talking to her like she's a dog. Dogs you can yell at because they respond when you're loud. Not your wife. Remember she is not psychic or a know it all, you have to explain yourself when asking something from your wife. Don't let her assume, because that will always lead to an argument. If not an argument at least hurt feelings. Hurt feelings=Anger. Remember that. Let me add that my buddy is no longer married. She divorced him and he never wanted to lose her.

Now let's change it up. What if she asks you to do something? This is what you should do: Get all the information you need to make sure you get what she wants. Did you know this is why women nag? That's it really. She has had things that forever she thought you would get done and at one point she snaps. That's when the nagging starts. Let's use the dishes as an example. Of course she's been nagging to you about doing the dishes, and geez louis can't she just shut up! First off the reason she's nagging you about it is that you never do them. Have you washed dishes before or put them in the dishwasher? I have and it sucks. You don't think it sucks for her too? Cause it does. So anyways do freaking dishes every once in a while. Before you do though make sure you communicate to her. Something like this, "Okay I'm gonna do the dishes. If you need me to do something specific with them you need to tell me now before I start, because if not I'm going to do it my way. Cause I don't want to get mad when I'm done because you start telling me everything that I did wrong."

See how easy that is? Cover your ass before you do something for her and that way she can't get mad at you. Ask her what she wants, specifically, because you are not a psychic either.

Details my friend. They can save you a world of hurt. Just because you've know each other for so long does not mean you should take your communication for granted. Explain yourself to her. She's deserves it.

I'm going to share with you something a little extra. This was one of the things that used to get me angry at my wife. We'd decide to go eat at the Pancake House. Their food is delicious. We were on our way there when she said something like this, "Mimi's Cafe sounds good too though." Me, thinking that I had to please my wife would oblige and go to Mimi's. I'd be pissed the whole time eating there and afterwards at her. Why? Because I'm a guy and once we make a decision we don't tend to not break from it. That morning my mission was to get us to the Pancake House, and somewhere along the way I was deviated from that. Add to that I really wanted Pancake House. I could already taste their Swedish pancakes. Yet when my wife just made a suggestion, not really caring about where we went, I decided to oblige. Like an idiot I would get mad at her. There was no good reason to get mad at her, but I did. Simply because she took away my Swedish pancakes, and I thought I had to be a good husband and give her Mimi's. That line of thinking is idiotic. So she and I realized that I would get angry about stuff like this. It had happened more then once.

What I did to fix this problem was just tell her what I wanted. I wouldn't let her be a psychic. The crazy part was she never cared if we went to Mimi's or not, she was just talking. It was me that would get wrapped around it and get angry about it. Being the "great" husband is not about giving your wife everything that comes out of her mouth. Sometimes she's just saying stuff to say stuff. Communicate to her what you really want, whether it's pancakes or a having another kid. Just make sure to communicate so that ultimately you don't get angry and hurt her.

5. The Lecture problem

Let me start this chapter by giving the dictionary's definition on the word lecture. It is, "a speech of warning or reproof as to conduct; a long, tedious reprimand.". I really do not understand why we do this, and WE ALL do this. All husbands for some reason lecture their wives. You know what I say to this? SHUT UP!!! Enough with the lecturing[1] already. She's a grown woman you don't have to talk to her like she's a 6 year old. This will grate on women so much that at one point she won't share anything with you.

Have you ever wondered why your wife doesn't share with you anymore? How come she will share with her friends but not with you? This is the reason! Everytime she's tried to share with you about something, you decide to give her a lecture on how she should go about dealing with whatever she's dealing with. Still don't get it? Let me give a couple of examples.

The first example is my friend who decided to tell his wife how to lose weight. LMAO, I'm sorry, I can't stop laughing thinking of this. What the heck was he thinking?? I don't know but anyways let's get back to the example. So how does he do it? He get's some books on losing weight sits her at the table and begins to lecture her. He talks about how the info in these books are going to help her, and he tells her how eating six meals a day is the only way to lose weight, plus how she needs to watch her carb intake...and blah blah blah. Just spewing information and having her sit there having to listen to him. I think he spoke to her for like 40 mins straight. She barely said anything. You know what? She didn't do a damn thing he had told her. Why? Because first off who want's to

---

[1] This phenomenon of lecturing was revealed to me in Gary Smalley's book, *If Only He Knew What No Woman Can Resist*

listen to a lecture in their own house? I've paid good money for professors in college to lecture me, but I don't need it in my house. Neither does your wife.

Now on the topic of an overweight wife, which some of you may have. Lecturing her about losing weight is not the way to go about having her get thinner. The first thing is being a man that she respects. If she doesn't respect you forget it, she ain't losing weight. She doesn't want to be fat, but who does she have to look good for? Not you because she can't respect you. If you use the tools in this book though she will grow her respect for you.

So what should have my friend done? Let's just say that she does respect him, which as far as I know she does. This is what that conversation should have looked like. "Babe, I'm a little worried. I want you too be happy but you don't seem to happy about the way you look. You've told me that you're overweight and how it really bothers you. So what can I do to help?" From there let her talk and DON'T interrupt. Just let her talk. She probably knows what she needs to do and if not then you can recommend something. This is how you should recommend, "Well do you think if we (I used the word "we" not "you". That means the two of you are in it together) bought some books it would help? Or would you like to do some kind of weight loss plan? Whatever you choose I want you to know that I want to help you in any way I can. If it means I need to pick up the kids or change my schedule, I'll do it. I want you to be happy." Do you notice that I made it so that you would have to take on some responsibility? Cause you do. If you want your wife to lose weight/ or some other endeavor you can't just think it's gonna happen. You have to put in work.

Now some of you may think it sounds sappy. It's not you freaking blockhead. That's how you show tenderness to your wife. Once you can learn how to treat her with tenderness she will respond.

Actually a few words about tenderness. I teach a marriage seminar called Hammer & Roses. There's an explanation for the name of it. Men are like hammers. Hammers are excellent tools. Just about everything that is built around you had to have a hammer to do it. They are used to do projects around the house, hang up pictures and especially build homes. Women are like Roses. They are beautiful and they make a house a home. Here's the problem. A hammer is a very blunt object. Without even thinking about it you can break something very easily with it. With roses if you don't handle them carefully they will prick you with their sharp thorns. Men/ Hammer's think that they can talk and treat their wives like a piece of 2x4. Just hammer a little here and a little there and she should make this house work. The force of this hammer will use anger and lecture to get her to fit. Then as they do this they get surprised when their wives unleash the thorns. Because if you don't handle a rose with care it will prick you. Unfortunately at one point the rose will begin to wilt and not look anything like the beauty that it was before. Simply because it was treated with blunt force.

Tenderness fixes this. With tenderness alone you can bring a rose back. It can take a long time before it's brilliance shines again, but with constant tenderness it will shine again.

Alright another point about lecturing. It means that you don't have to fix everything. If she's telling you about a struggle she's going through, don't jump into the conversation and tell her how to fix it!!! This is a big lecture problem. See, because that's how men talk. If you come up to me and tell me that you have a problem with your car. I'll listen and then tell you what your best options would be to fix it. Something like, "Well I know a mechanic that can fix that." or "Did you check to see if the battery was connected correctly?" maybe even "Heck all that probably needs is a new alternator." We guys try to fix our problems. That's just what we do and how we talk. If you tell me about a struggle you're going through, I'm going to tell you my opinion on the best way to fix it. This is not always the case with women! All they really want most of the time is for you just to listen. That's it. Then once she's done ask her open-ended questions. Like this, "Well what do you think you're going to do?" "That sounds tough. Do you need my help?". Obviously if she has car problems then try to fix it, but I'm sure you get my point. All she really wants is for you to listen and empathize with her.

     Before I close up this chapter I want to give a personal example. A few years ago I came home and Amy told me she had a headache. It had lasted all day and was driving her crazy. When I asked her what she had taken for it she told me she hadn't taken anything. What the heck? You see Amy is not too keen on taking medicine. She's a Marine that way. Anyways my response was a textbook example of lecturing, "Why haven't you taken anything? You mean you've decided to sit in the house all day with this pain? What are you thinking? That should have been the first thing you should have done. That's crazy to be in that kind of pain....and I'm completely lecturing you. You're in pain and I'm lecturing you. I'm sorry. Let me help." At that point I grabbed some Tylenol for her, which she was willing to take, and a glass of orange juice. I helped her on the couch to lie down and take a nap. I then went upstairs to get on the computer so I wouldn't make any noise while she rested. Actions instead of words make a huge difference when showing tenderness.

6. The Marriage-Killer

I'm going to tell you about the true cancer that kills marriages. The reason I call it cancer is because it starts off small. It starts off slowly but by the end it envelops everything by fully killing the relationship.

Ignoring your wife.

That right there friends is the main cause for divorce. Let me explain. I'll start off with an example of your daily routine:
1. Wake up, drink coffee/eat breakfast, some small talk with family, go to work.
2. Work, Eat Lunch, Go Home. Maybe a quick phone call to pick up milk on the way home.
3. Get home, change your clothes, maybe go take the kids to practice, and then eat dinner.
4. Watch some TV, movie, or get on the internet/play some video games, talk a little about your day to your wife. She tells you about some stuff also.
5. Go to sleep, and start all over again the next day.
6. On the weekend hang out with family and friends. Just taking it easy.

Sounds normal right? At first look there doesn't seem anything wrong with it, especially for men. That looks like a solid week, and you were damn productive too. Went to work, helped the kids at practice, and finished it with a relaxing weekend...which at no time did you value your wife. Did you take her to the park for a stroll? How about get her a card? Tell her that you are proud of her? Touch her? Did you do the dishes?

Probably not, and that is how you ignore your wife. The

examples I gave above are from a great book called, *The Five Love Languages*[2], by Gary Chapman. I'll talk about them in a little bit, but first let me explain why ignoring your wife will kill your marriage.

There are two main factors that come into play when you ignore your wife. The first being growth. You see humans are always growing. We don't ever stop learning. When your wife attached herself to you, it's because she knew that she wanted to grow with you. Once you begin to ignore her, she stops growing. Now I'm not saying that she can't learn on her own, but YOU are getting in the way of her learning. You have basically started to stifle her growth, because she can't share anything with you. Ignoring her makes her believe, which is true, that her husband does not care about her daily life. We as men never think of it. NEVER. We think it's all good because the house looks fine and dinner was on the table. Were hammers that way. Think about it, she wants to grow and share with you all her thoughts and ideas. If you don't ask though, she won't tell you. I mean sometimes she might tell you, but all she gets is a "Uh-huh". Now let me show you a tool on how to listen to your wife.

Tell her this, "Alright lets sit down and tell me what's up. For the next 30-mins/hour you have my undivided attention. Just realize I can only go for so long. I want to talk but you know I can only go for so long.", be honest and direct with her. Like I wrote earlier, cover your ass, when communicating to your wife. This should be done at least twice a week. It can also be done on a date night. Let me be very clear on this: YOU NEED TO HAVE A DATE NIGHT WITH YOUR WIFE. At least twice a month. Remember date night doesn't always mean something grand. It can be going to Starbucks drinking coffee and hanging out, or going to the

---

2 This book should be in every couples inventory.

beach or the park. Also it doesn't mean that the two of you have to be talking the whole time. Trust me all she wants is to have you close to her for a little while.

If you do not listen to your wife, she will stop growing for you. She might grow for herself but not for you. This means that you will lose your wife because you have no investment in her life. To invest in someone's life means work.

Ok I said there are two factors that come into play when you ignore your wife. The second being: **other men**. That's right men. You see we live in an age that Facebook, Twitter, Myspace and all other kinds of social networks exist. Example time. I have friend who lost his wife to X-Box live. Go ahead and reread that if you have to, and let it set in. This is what happened. She, being ignored, for who knows how long, had become a very wilted rose. No investment from her husband, which means no tenderness. So her son says, "Mom you got to see this it's so cool. You can play on-line with other people! Here look put on the headset.", so she starts to play, because she actually liked the game.

As time went on though something happened. If you've ever played on-line games you know that very little women play. Once a bunch of guys playing heard the voice of a woman playing also they all became Casanova's. That is a very different experience for a middle-aged women. All of a sudden a ton of guys are giving her a lot of attention. Attention that she was not getting at all from her husband. Also if you've been on the internet the attention is over the top. So what does she do? She starts talking more and more to this one specific guy. She adds him as a friend and before you know it she's on Xbox-Live everyday. This little on-line game relationship grows so big that at last she leaves her husband. She leaves him for someone who is not ignoring her.

You want to call her a "slut" don't you? We men think

that women need to stand beside us through thick and thin, but then we completely ignore her...and other men don't. What do you think she was going to do? Stick around with the guy that's been ignoring her for the last five years of a fifteen year marriage? Hell no, and you wouldn't either. Maybe before when technological communication was not as great women wouldn't leave their husbands. Simply because there was no one around to give them attention. Well let me give you a heads up: Shit's changed.

    Our lives are bombarded everyday with communication, especially social networking. Plus your wife probably works. You're telling me that there isn't some dude right now that wouldn't try to put the moves on your wife? Cause there is and you know it as well as I do. They don't see her with the faults that you see her with. They see her with all the great qualities that you saw when you first met her. And if you don't give her the attention and love that she deserves, someone else will.

    Don't get me wrong. If she leaves she's in the wrong, but don't think for one second you had nothing to do with it. If you were the husband that you should have been she will/would never leave.

    Man up. You have a responsibility as a husband. Stop ignoring a woman who wants to live her life with you. Ignoring your wife has grave consequences. The next chapter will be about how to stop ignoring her.

7. Showing love

The best way to ignore your wife is to not show her love...duh. Now here's the thing, we all don't love the same. Remember towards the beginning of the book I said I would explain why you think you treat your wife good, but you're actually not. Let me clear that up. The best way is to give an example.

Personally I feel loved when my wife tells me, "You are a great father." or let's say I'm going through something difficult, "You are going to do great. I know you will because you're amazing.". Obviously everyone feels good when someone says something nice to them, but I literally feel "loved" this way. On the other hand, I can tell Amy she's the best wife in the whole world until I'm blue in the face, and she'll thank me, but doesn't get much out of it. Do you have any idea how much this infuriated me when I was first married?? How can she not like it when I tell her something nice? I thought there was something wrong with her or maybe it was me. She never seemed to even care when I did tell her something nice. Reason being that Words of Affirmation was not the way she felt loved, at all. My wife's primary love language is Quality Time.

Once we figured this out literally everything changed. She now felt loved which in turn also brings trust and patience. So what did I do to give her quality time? This is one of the ways that I give her quality time: About once to three times a week we go the park. It's right down the road from where I live. We take our son and he runs around playing while she and I spend time together. Sometimes we talk and sometimes we don't. What matters is that I spend time with her and there are no other distractions.

At home I can't pull it off as easily simply because the internet, TV, computer games, or whatever else that comes up gets in the way. Sometimes after our son falls asleep we sit together drink wine and hang out, this is also quality time for her. Because I spend quality time with her my relationship runs smoothly with her. I'm keeping her love tank full.

Let me list the Love Languages so we can all be on the same page:
1. Quality Time
2. Words of Affirmation
3. Receiving Gifts
4. Acts of Service
5. Physical Touch

Now let me give you an example of why you may think you're treating your wife good, but actually not. If you get home with roses and chocolates (Receiving Gifts) but your wife doesn't seem to give a damn it's probably because she doesn't feel love that way! On the other hand if you were to clean her car (Acts of Service) she just might jump on top of you. Yet if you're not getting her love language right she will not be happy with you. Add to the fact that she's probably not loving you the way you like. She's making sandwich after sandwich and folding all your clothes (Acts of Service) trying to show you love. When in reality you just want her to rub your neck (Physical Touch) because that is when you feel love. Crazy huh? All that time spending it with that person and not having a clue on how to love them. This is why I highly recommend getting *The Five Love Languages* by Gary Chapman. It goes into great detail on how to figure out and show these love languages.

With that said, once you learn how to show love to your wife you will no longer be ignoring her. This begins the foundation for a healthy and strong marriage.

8. The WIIFM

Okay so you've gone this far with me. Some of you may be saying, "Okay Orlando this sounds cool and all, but What's In It For Me (WIIFM)?" Well obviously you're no longer going home to a house of craziness. These tools makes your marriage into a good one. Let me quote my sister on having a bad marriage, "Having a bad marriage is like having diarrhea everyday.", and she's right. Dude it sucks waking up in the morning knowing that at one point in the day the two of you are going to fight. Why even be married? Really who wants to go through that crap? So the first WIIFM is that peace can begin to live in your house if you use these tools.

But wait there's more!

Once she feels loved, trust and patience comes with it. This means it makes it much easier to pursue our passion. See just about every guy I know has a passion. It can be surfing, running, model trains, role-playing games, MMA, reading and the list goes on and on. Your wife, once she feels that she is loved will give you time. She knows you're not going anywhere and she knows that she is first in your life. For me this is how it translates. I do Brazilian Jiu-Jitsu. I train just about everyday (five to six days a week) about two hours a day. That's a ton of training! Jiu-Jitsu is my passion but if I wasn't loving my wife the way I should it would be impossible to train. Simply because she'd question me every time I'd go. I'd hear things like, "Oh you love training more then you love me!" or "Am I not as special??". I know for a fact some of you guys get these comments. So let me tell you the next WIIFM: If you love your wife right, she will encourage your passion.

Let me add something though. If at any time Amy says

to me, "I want you to stay home tonight." I never tell her no. Why? Because she deserves my time. She's an awesome wife and she has to know that she is always in first place.

What about sex? It's pretty important for a marriage. I have sex as much as a I want. That means for me it's about 2-3 times a week. Some of you may think that's a lot where others may think that's too little. What matters is that I get laid pretty much whenever I want. That is a blessing for me. A lot of wives do not want to have sex with their husbands because they constantly have their feelings hurt. The last WIIFM: Your sex life will get better once you start treating your wife better.

Now this all doesn't happen overnight but it will happen. Using the tools, which may seem cumbersome at first, will eventually give you freedom.

9. Numero #1!

Alright let's talk about you, Mr. Numero #1. What can you do for yourself to make your own life better?
For starters it's this: If work is not letting you enjoy life, it may be time for a change. You may be saying, "But work benefits my livelihood!", and it does but not always your sanity. I mean really how many freaking Saturday Morning Specials or movies do you need to get the point across. WORKING ALL THE TIME DOES NOT BRING HAPPINESS! Stuff ultimately is not going to give you happiness. Heck how are you going to enjoy it if you can only enjoy it when you go on your one week vacation per year? The answer is you won't enjoy it. Man, you really need to make a change in your daily routine to bring joy to your life. Don't get stuck in the rat race.

Now if you're some twenty-two year old kid with no family, which then I don't understand why you're reading this book, work all you want. In general though most of us are not.

If all you do is work...life probably sucks. Also your wife wants to be with you. Really. Right now she may think you're an asshole, but once you start showing tenderness she is going to want to be with you. If work is always taking you away from her, then seriously consider your alternatives.

10. Hobby

Life goes quick. Real quick. So find a way to enjoy it. For starters find a hobby. It doesn't have to be a passion but something that you can enjoy on a daily basis. It can be following sports, reading, learning a new language, boating, fishing, guitar, and the list goes on and on. Most of you know what you already like. Just delve into it a little deeper. This way you have a way to release and forget about life for a little while. Some people may say that's not responsible. I say that they can suck it. A hobby or passion is YOUR TIME. If you can do it 2-3 times a week it's perfect. I have a friend whose hobby is carpentry. He tells me that he loves sitting in his garage working on something for an hour. That it's just an hour brings some "me-time" into his life. Another example would be to join a softball team. You get to hang out with friends and enjoy a game. Like I said, it doesn't have to be long and arduous. It just has to be something that you enjoy. For all you may know that hobby can become a passion.

11. Working Out

Okay this is not so much a tool that I know works because it has logic behind it. This is something that I believe in my gut. I believe every man needs to physically workout. ALL MEN. What I mean by that is doing an exercise-related activity that pushes your body. We as men NEED to workout.

It's in us to fight, and most of the time there isn't anyone there to fight. This is why you need to fight yourself! You are your biggest enemy. The best way to deal with that anger is to workout.

For myself I do Brazilian Jiu-Jitsu. It fulfills my passion and workout criteria. When I didn't have Jiu-Jitsu I did Crossfit in my garage. Crossfit is a method of working out by doing exercises from different aerobic and anaerobic activities.

That doesn't mean you need to do Crossfit, but you do need to push your body. I know that there are some of you out there right now saying, "But Orlando I'm a wimp or fatass." I don't care! This is the best way to deal with the anger monster inside of you. So let me give you a list of some great ways to workout.

1. Crossfit: Just Google it and see if there are any gyms nearby. It can be kind of expensive at times so you can actually do it in your garage. That's what I did. This will kick your ass though. The Crossfit mascot is Pukie the clown. It's because Crossfit will probably make you puke the first time you do it. It's tough but very rewarding.
2. Running: Nothing like running. Bruce Lee said it was the king of exercises. Also it's free! Just put some sneakers on and go.
3. Swim: Find a pool and swim. Take lessons if you need to.
4. Muay Thai Kickboxing: Nothing better then to hit something to make you feel better. Also just because you train kickboxing does not mean you have to spar. Look for a good gym with good instructors and tell them your goals. It's also a great way to shed fat very fast.
5. Brazilian Jiu-Jitsu: Of course I was going to list it. It's

not for everyone though and it can give you really ugly ears. It's a great way to stay in shape, learn self-defense, and let out some steam.
6. Bike-riding: Either street or mountain is excellent.
7. Climbing: I don't do it that much anymore but it will get you really strong. I mostly did it indoors. Most indoor gyms offer memberships. Sign up. Learn. Climb.
8. Join a gym: This is my last recommendation simply because I don't like gyms. I think it's because I'm not as challenged or because the music sucks most of the time. Either way it's still a place where you can lift some iron and pack on some muscle. If you can find a workout partner it makes it much more rewarding.

Here are some links you can check out:
www.crossfit.com
www.rosstraining.com

At rosstraining.com you can get a lot of info on how to workout hard at home.

Gents you need to workout. Also I don't mean golf or most sports. I think golf is a great hobby or passion, but not for a hard workout. It has to be something that is heart-pounding and by the time you're done you're sweating buckets. Don't believe that lie in your head that you are too weak or too fat. It will help you out tremendously in dealing with your anger. Not to mention that it will help out your health.

12. Re: Cheating

Alright you probably thought I wasn't going to talk about this. Gotcha! Okay first off let me say that all guys are capable of cheating. ALL OF THEM. You know why? Because you have a dick. That's it. Respect the power of your penis because it can get you in a world of pain. Dude our dicks will do the most outlandish things. Even worse if were drinking or adding any kind of drug to our body. Forget it! We completely lose our way and let our dicks do the thinking. So let's talk about how not to cheat.

First off don't put yourself in a place where you might be tempted to cheat. For instance, when Amy was deployed to Iraq I would watch where I went. I had a buddy of mine that asked me to go to Tijuana with him to go party. He didn't ask me because he wanted me to cheat on my wife. He wanted me to go so I could have fun and get out of the house. He asked with the best of intentions. Problem is that it was to Tijuana!! If I had gone the tequila whistle guy would have become my best friend. Do you know what I would have done in TJ once I got drunk?? Me neither and that's why I didn't go. I don't trust myself in that environment. I'm not writing this book because I'm a saint. I'm writing this book because I know how hard it can be to be a good husband. This is why if you want to be a good husband watch where you go. It could be a little party, at the local bar, or over the house of your next door neighbor that is asking for help with her garbage disposal. Keep your eyes open and think ahead of the consequences. Remember you can cheat because you have a dick.

Now let's say you've already cheated and your wife knows. The next step is to regain her trust. Use the tools this book teaches. Yet you will also have to become an open book. Let her look through your phone, emails, Facebook or anything else that can carry information. She needs to regain trust and the best way is to show her that you have nothing to hide. Also call and check in with her. It sounds stupid but it keeps her feeling safe that you aren't out cheating on her. This is a long road by the way. It can take a while before she regains trust in you. Keep it up though and make it work.

    Now if you've cheated and she doesn't know....this can get sticky. Maybe you cheated on your wife and the second it happened you realized something: NEVER AGAIN WOULD YOU DO THAT. It just was not worth it and your wife is perfect compared to the girl you were with. Sometimes it takes a really stupid mistake to see how great you have it. In this case I'd recommend not telling her. Oh I know I'm going to get a lot of crap for that. Yet sometimes ignorance is bliss. Here's the deal. Get back on the right track and show your wife love. Also if you are feeling that you need to tell her, then tell her. The truth can set you free! Although if the feelings of wanting to cheat come back, then tell her or get counseling. You have to man. That's no way to live a married life. Plus you are completely hurting/ disrespecting her.

    On the other hand if you have an ongoing relationship with another woman; you need to tell your wife ASAP. Tell her right now if you have to. Cause that will bite you in the ass in a BIG way. If you have kids, a nice house, and perfect little life, kiss it all goodbye if she finds out you're cheating. That is some serious pain. That you nor she want to go through. Once you decide to tell her there are a few ways of doing it. You can do it one on one. If you have the courage for it this is a good way to tell her. Now if you're kinda scared go to a counselor. It's okay to be scared. Having a mediator when you tell her will give you some strength. Also it might have her give you a chance because you are willing to seek help. Either way it's going to be tough.

Watching out for Number #1 can be tough at first. You have to make sacrifices just for yourself. Become a better man though. Life's short. Take it by the reigns and live it.

13. Let's wrap it up!

I'm gonna make this ending short and sweet. So just hang in there.

Gent's, I know I've gone through a lot of information with you. I also realize I could have really gone into the weeds with this stuff. That's not the point. The point of this book is to make you move. To take action in your marriage. Heck when you use these tools for the first time they might come out all wrong. Good, cause at least you're trying. Don't lose your marriage and look back with regret. Everybody that gets divorced does that. Make a difference and don't be a statistic. Dare to be different. We live in a world that lies to us, and tells us that marriages can't make it. Give that lie the middle-finger. The only way to do that is to take your marriage into your own hands. It's hard work so be ready. The great thing is that the rewards are immeasurable.

Don't give up, don't give up, don't give up.

Bibliography:

Chapman, Gary D. *The 5 Love Languages: the Secret to Love That Lasts*. Chicago: Northfield Pub., 2010. Print.

Smalley, Gary. *If Only He Knew What No Woman Can Resist*. Grand Rapids, MI: Zondervan Pub. House, 1996. Print.

Made in the USA
San Bernardino, CA
09 March 2013